Great Social Studies Projects™

The Birth and Growth of a Nation

Hands-on Projects About Symbols of American Liberty

Jennifer Quasha

The Rosen Publishing Group's
PowerKids Press™
New York

Some of the projects in this book were designed for a child to do together with an adult.

For Todd, in memory of the days filled with playing cowgirls and Indians.

Published in 2001 by The Rosen Publishing Group, Inc.
29 East 21st Street, New York, NY 10010

First Edition

Book Design: Felicity Erwin

Layout: Michael de Guzman

Photo Credits: p. 4 © SuperStock; pp. 6–21 by Pablo Maldonado.

Quasha, Jennifer.
    The birth and growth of a nation : hands-on projects about symbols of American liberty / Jennifer Quasha.
      p. cm.— (Great social studies projects)
    Includes index.
    Summary: This book is an introduction to the birth of a nation, the United States of America, and the symbols that sprang up as the nation grew, with instructions for models of the Liberty Bell, the Statue of Liberty, the bald eagle, and others.
    ISBN 0-8239-5703-9
    1.Emblems, National—Study and teaching—Activity programs—Juvenile literature. [1. Emblems, National. 2. Handicraft.] I. Title. II. Series.

JC346. Q37 2000
929.9'2'0973—dc21   00-029809

Manufactured in the United States of America

Contents

Birth and Growth of a Nation

In 1776, America became **independent** from England. Up until then, England had ruled the American **colonies**. This meant that the people living in America had to follow English laws. By winning the **Revolutionary War**, America won its independence. In 1776, the **Declaration of Independence** was written and signed. The United States of America was born. As this new country grew, many **symbols** sprang up. A symbol is an object or design that stands for something important. Early symbols of the United States stood for freedom and strength. People put these symbols on everyday objects. The symbols helped them remember what was important to them.

Here's a picture that shows Independence Hall in Philadelphia, Pennsylvania, in 1776. The Declaration of Independence was born in this historic building.

Liberty Bell Model

In 1752, the English sent a large bell to America. The bell was to celebrate the founding of the colony of Pennsylvania, one of the first American colonies, over 50 years before. The bell was to be used in front of the new State House in Philadelphia, Pennsylvania. The first time the bell was rung, it cracked. There was a quote about **liberty engraved** on the bell. It said: "Proclaim liberty throughout all the land unto all the inhabitants thereof…." The bell was called the Liberty Bell because of this quote. Here's how to make your own Liberty Bell:

| tools and materials | • yellow plastic cup
• scissors
• piece of string
• bell
• black marker |

6

1 Poke a small hole into the top of the cup with the scissors.

2 Make a loop with the string and tie a knot small enough to fit through the hole in the cup. Tie bell to the bottom of the string.

3 Thread the loop through the hole in the cup so the bell stays under the cup and the loop is above.

4 Draw the crack with the marker.

The Great Seal

The Great Seal is on the American dollar bill. It was designed between 1776 and 1782. It is a two-sided seal. It has a bald eagle on one side. The eagle holds arrows and olive branches. Across its chest is a shield with 13 stripes. The stripes stand for the first 13 American colonies. There is a banner in the eagle's mouth and stars above its head. The other side of the seal has a **pyramid**, which stands for strength. The eye above stands for the "all-seeing" power of God. Here's how to make the Great Seal:

tools and materials

- piece of poster board at least 4" x 8" (10 x 20 cm)
- scissors
- one dollar bill
- pencil
- green and black markers

Cut out a 4" x 8" (10 x 20 cm) piece of poster board.

 Put a dollar bill next to the piece of poster board. With the pencil, sketch onto the poster board all the objects you see on the bill, including the Great Seal.

 Color in your bill with the green and black markers.

Pair of American Flag Place Mats

Today's American flag has 13 stripes, 6 white ones and 7 red ones. These stripes stand for the first 13 American colonies. The flag also has a blue square with 50 white stars inside of it. These stars stand for the 50 states that make up the United States today. The first American flag did not look this way. It had the red and white stripes, but instead of the blue part with white stars, it had a small English flag. It was called the Grand Union Flag. Here's how to make American flag place mats:

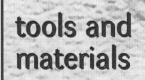

tools and materials

- piece of red felt at least 19" x 24" (48 x 61 cm)
- piece of white felt at least 9" x 12" (23 x 31 cm)
- piece of blue felt at least 11" x 12" (28 x 31 cm)
- scissors
- double-sided tape

Cut two pieces of red felt, 12" x 9 1/2" (31 x 24 cm) each. Cut six pieces of white felt, 1/2" x 12" (1.3 x 31 cm) each. Cut eight pieces of white felt 1/2" x 6" (1.3 x 15 cm) each.

 Tape white strips onto the two rectangles of red felt as shown. Notice where the longer pieces go and where the shorter ones should be placed.

 Cut two pieces of blue felt, 6 1/2" x 5 1/2" (16.5 x 14 cm) each. Cut out small stars from the white felt.

4 Tape the stars onto the two blue felt pieces. Tape blue felt pieces to red felt pieces.

Bald Eagle Paper Bird

The bald eagle is one of the world's largest birds. It is about three feet (0.9 m) tall. Its wingspan, the distance from the tip of one wing to the tip of the other, is about seven feet (2 m). This bird is seen as a symbol of strength because of its large size. In 1782, the bald eagle was chosen to be the **national** bird of the newly formed United States. Today the bald eagle can be seen on United States **currency**. Currency includes bills, coins, and banknotes. Here's how to make your own bald eagle:

tools and materials

- four brown, one white, and one yellow piece of construction paper
- scissors
- black pen
- clear tape
- rubber band
- strip of cardboard

1 Draw and cut out the shapes of the eagle's body and a wing from the brown paper. Cut the head shape and tail feathers from the white paper. Cut the shapes of the beak and a claw from the yellow paper. Trace all the shapes again and cut out a second one of every shape. You will have two body shapes, two wings, two heads, two beaks, and two claws.

2 Tape each of the pairs of shapes together, like a mirror image.

3 Cut rubber band and tape it to the underside of the eagle's body. Pull the band up through the space between the two body shapes.

4 On the underside of the eagle, tape a strip of cardboard across the body and down the eagle's wings.

A Quill Pen

The quill pen was the most popular writing tool in eighteenth-century America. It was often made from a goose feather. After being plucked, the **shaft** of the feather was carved so it could hold ink. The tip was carved into a sharp point for writing. A person had to dip the quill pen into a jar of ink in order to write. The ink was made from berries, squid ink, or a natural **mineral** called carbon. The Declaration of Independence was signed with a quill pen. Here's how to make your own quill pen:

tools and materials

- feather
- masking tape
- new, unsharpened pencil
- pencil sharpener

Tape the feather onto the back end of the pencil (the part with the eraser).

 Tape it again to make sure it's on tight and won't fall off.

 Sharpen the pencil and use it for writing.

Uncle Sam Yardstick Puppet

The War of 1812 was fought between the United States and England. A man named Sam Wilson owned the company that supplied the United States Army with meat. On each barrel of meat were the letters "U" and "S." Even though the letters stood for "United States," people started to say they stood for "Uncle Sam." Uncle Sam became a symbol of the United States Army. In 1830, Uncle Sam started to appear in cartoons as a man with a white beard, a blue coat, and red-and-white-striped pants. Here's how to make your own Uncle Sam:

tools and materials

- red, blue, and white felt (1/4 yard [23 cm] of each)
- scissors
- white cardboard
- skin-colored paint
- paintbrush
- black marker
- double-sided tape
- yardstick

Cut out from white felt a 6" x 4" (15 x 10 cm) rectangle for the hat, a 14" x 3" (36 x 8 cm) rectangle for the shirt, and a 7" x 4" (18 x 10 cm) rectangle for the stripes on the pants. From the blue felt, cut out a 9" x 10" (23 x 25 cm) rectangle for the jacket. From the red felt, cut out a 6" x 14" (15 x 36 cm) rectangle for the pants.

 From the leftover pieces of felt, cut out details like white stars, hair, a beard, cuffs, a red tie, and blue shoes. Cut an oval out of the cardboard that is 4" (10 cm) high and 3" (8 cm) wide.

 Paint the cardboard oval with the skin-colored paint. When paint is dry, add eyes, nose, and mouth with black marker.

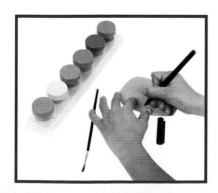

 Put double-sided tape on the felt details and stick them to the main pieces of clothing. Then put tape on the backs of the pieces of clothing. Stick the clothing onto the yardstick.

Statue of Liberty Clay Model

In 1886, France gave the Statue of Liberty to the United States. It was a gift to celebrate the **centennial**, or 100th birthday, of the United States. The Statue of Liberty is a statue of a woman called Lady Liberty. Lady Liberty wears a flowing robe and holds the torch of freedom in her right hand. In her left hand she holds a book with the date July 4, 1776, on it. This is the date the Declaration of Independence was signed. The Statue of Liberty stands in New York Harbor in New York City. Here's how to make your own Statue of Liberty:

tools and materials

- white modeling clay
- green and white paint
- paintbrush
- top of a small cardboard box
- white glue
- brown construction paper
- masking tape

Using white clay, mold the shape of Lady Liberty's body, head, and arms.

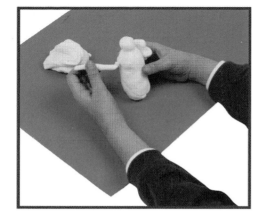

 Mold details like the torch, her crown, her hair, and the folds of her dress.

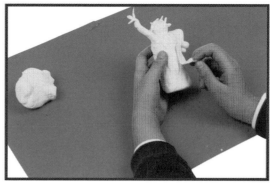

 Let clay dry overnight. When clay is dry, paint Lady Liberty light green. Mix green and white paint together to get the right shade. Let dry.

 Wrap box with brown paper and tape into place. Glue the Statue of Liberty to the box top, which will be her stand.

The Spirit of '76 Drum

The Spirit of '76 is the name of a large painting by Archibald Willard. He painted it to celebrate the centennial birthday of the United States in 1876. It soon became the most popular painting of the time. The painting shows three men wearing uniforms during the Revolutionary War. Two men are playing drums and the third is playing a **fife**, an instrument like a flute. Today this picture is seen as a symbol of America's fight for freedom. Here's how to make your own *Spirit of '76* drum:

tools and materials

- clean, empty tin can, top and bottom removed
- shoelace
- two large white balloons
- scissors
- masking tape
- 8 1/2" x 11" (22 x 28 cm) piece of white paper
- colored markers
- two new, unsharpened pencils

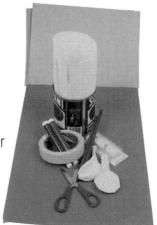

Thread the shoelace through the tin can and tie a knot.

 Cut the ends off two balloons.

 Stretch one balloon over one end of the can, and the second balloon over the other end. Tape balloons to the sides of the can.

 Cut the white paper so it's the right size to fit around the sides of the can. Decorate the paper and tape it around the can. Play the drum with the unsharpened pencils.

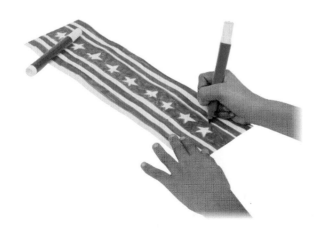

How to Use Your Projects

You have learned some important information about the birth, growth, and symbols of the United States of America. You have also made some great projects! There are many different things you can do with them. You can give your flag place mats to a friend or relative as a useful present. You can show your younger brother or sister how to play your *Spirit of '76* drum. You can use your Statue of Liberty model as part of a school project on American independence.

Your projects would also make nice decorations. Hang your bald eagle on the dining room wall for your Fourth of July dinner to help you and your family celebrate the birth of our nation. You can share all you have learned, along with your wonderful social studies projects, with your family and friends.

Glossary

centennial (sen-TEH-nee-ul) Having to do with the 100th anniversary.

colonies (KAH-luh-neez) Areas in a country where large groups of people move, who are still ruled by the leaders and laws of their old countries.

currency (KUR-en-see) The money that is in use in a country.

Declaration of Independence (deh-kluh-RAY-shun UV in-duh-PEN-dints) A paper signed on July 4, 1776, declaring that the American colonies were independent of England.

engraved (en-GRAYVD) Something that has been carved.

fife (FYF) A small flutelike instrument that you blow, with six to eight finger holes and no keys.

independent (in-dih-PEN-dint) Being able to think and do things for oneself.

liberty (LIH-ber-tee) Freedom.

mineral (MIH-ner-ul) A natural ingredient from Earth's soil, such as coal or copper, that comes from the ground and is not a plant, animal, or other living thing.

national (NAH-shuh-nul) Belonging to a country.

pyramid (PEER-uh-mid) A large stone structure with a square bottom and triangular sides.

Revolutionary War (reh-vuh-LOO-shuh-nayr-ee WOR) The war that American colonists fought from 1775 to 1783 to win independence from England.

shaft (SHAFT) A long, slender stem.

symbols (SIM-bulz) Objects or designs that stand for something important.

Index

Web Sites

To learn more about the birth and growth of the United States of America,
    check out this Web site:

http://www.earlyamerica.com